# THE ART OF QUESTIONING

Solve Problems, Spark Creativity, Resolve Conflicts, and Master the Ultimate Skill for Personal and Professional Growth

## PRADIP DAS

are declared or implied. Readers acknowledge that the author is not engaging in the rendering of legal, financial, medical or professional advice. The content within this book has been derived from various sources. Please consult a licensed professional before attempting any techniques outlined in this book.

By reading this document, the reader agrees that under no circumstances is the author responsible for any losses, direct or indirect, which are incurred as a result of the use of information contained within this document, including, but not limited to, — errors, omissions, or inaccuracies.

**Access Free Courses**

https://community.askpndas.com

# Table of Contents


Table of Contents ...................................................4

Introduction.........................................................5

The Psychology of Questions .....................................11

Types of Questions ..................................................24

Crafting the Perfect Question .................................36

Asking the Right Questions ...................................44

Questioning Techniques for Different Situations .......52

Exploring Assumptions ...........................................63

Questioning for Problem Solving ...........................72

Eliciting Deep Insights...........................................80

Leading Through Questions ...................................89

Enhancing Learning Through Questions ................. 100

Understanding Client Needs ................................. 110

Building a Questioning Mindset............................. 120

Overcoming Common Mistakes............................. 131

Becoming a Questioning Expert............................. 143

Conclusion ......................................................... 151

# Introduction

A man walks barefoot through the busy streets of Athens, stopping to talk with people from all walks of life. He's not selling anything or preaching. Instead, he's asking questions. This man is Socrates, and his questions would change the world.

Socrates believed that the path to wisdom began with admitting how little we truly know. His method was simple yet powerful - ask questions that make people think deeply about their beliefs and assumptions. He didn't claim to have all the answers. Instead, he showed that asking the right questions could lead to greater understanding.

This book is about the power of questions. Like Socrates, we can use questions to learn, to solve problems, and to see the world in new ways. Good questions can spark creativity, challenge old ideas, and open up new possibilities.

You might be wondering, "Why do we need a book about questions? Isn't asking questions something we all do naturally?" It's true that we all ask questions, but not all questions are created equal. Some questions can change lives, start movements, or lead to groundbreaking discoveries. Others fall flat or lead us down the wrong path.

The Power of Questions

Questions are more than just a way to get information. They're tools that can shape our thinking and change the world around us. Let's look at some ways questions can be powerful:

Questions spark curiosity: When we ask "Why?" or "How?", we open doors to new knowledge. A single good question can lead to a lifetime of learning and discovery.

Questions challenge assumptions: By asking "Is this really true?" or "What if we tried something different?", we can break free from old ways of thinking and find new solutions.

Questions build connections: Asking someone about their experiences or thoughts can create understanding and empathy. Good questions are at the heart of meaningful conversations and relationships.

Questions drive innovation: Many of the world's greatest inventions started with a simple question. "What if we could...?" has led to countless breakthroughs in science, technology, and other fields.

Questions promote critical thinking: When we ask "How do we know this?" or "What's the evidence?", we learn to think more clearly and avoid being misled by false information.

Questions empower us: By asking "How can I make a difference?" or "What's the next step?", we take control of our lives and become active shapers of our world, not just passive observers.

Throughout this book, we'll explore these different aspects of questioning. You'll learn how to ask questions that inspire, inform, and lead to positive change. Whether you're a student, a professional, or just someone who wants to understand the world better, mastering the art of questioning can help you achieve your goals and live a richer, more engaged life.

Why Questioning Matters

Questions are the engines of human progress. They drive us to explore, innovate, and understand. Think about some of the biggest breakthroughs in history:

"What if the Earth isn't the center of the universe?" This question led Copernicus to reshape our understanding of the cosmos.

"Why do apples fall straight down?" Isaac Newton's curiosity about this simple event paved the way for his theory of gravity.

"What makes people sick?" This question has driven medical advances that have saved millions of lives.

These examples show that questions can change the world. But questioning isn't just for scientists and philosophers. It's a skill that can improve every part of our lives.

Good questions can:

Solve problems: When faced with a challenge, the right questions can help us find solutions we might otherwise miss.

Improve relationships: Asking thoughtful questions shows we care and helps us understand others better.

Boost learning: Questions keep our minds active and help us remember information longer.

Spark creativity: A well-framed question can lead to new ideas and innovations.

Make better decisions: By questioning our assumptions and gathering information, we can make smarter choices.

Despite these benefits, many of us don't use questions as well as we could. We might fear looking foolish, or we might be so focused on finding answers that we don't take time to ask good questions. Sometimes, we simply don't know how to ask the kinds of questions that lead to breakthroughs.

That's where this book comes in. In the chapters ahead, we'll look at different types of questions, when to use them, and how to craft questions that get results. We'll also explore common barriers to effective questioning and how to overcome them.

By the end of this book, you'll have a toolkit of questioning techniques to use in all areas of your life. More importantly, you'll develop a questioning mindset — a curiosity about the world and a willingness to challenge assumptions, including your own.

So, are you ready to unlock the power of questions in your life? Let's get started.

# The Psychology of Questions

The Psychology of Questions Understanding the Human Mind How Questions Influence Thinking

Questions are more than just a way to get information. They shape how we think, feel, and act. To become better at asking questions, it helps to understand how our brains respond to them. In this chapter, we'll explore the psychology behind questions and how they influence our minds.

The Curious Brain

Humans are naturally curious. From the time we're babies, we explore the world around us, touching, tasting, and asking endless "why" questions. This curiosity is built into our brains.

When we encounter a question, our brains light up. Scientists have found that questions activate the parts of our brain involved in memory, problem-solving, and reward. In other words, our brains like questions. They see them as puzzles to solve.

This is why a good question can be so engaging. It creates a gap in our knowledge that our brain wants to fill. It's like an itch we need to scratch. This "information gap" theory, proposed by George Loewenstein, explains why we find it hard to stop reading a mystery novel or why we keep scrolling through our social media feeds. We want to know what happens next.

But not all questions are created equal in the eyes of our brains. Questions that are too easy or too hard don't engage us as much. The sweet spot is a question that's challenging but not impossible. It needs to be within reach of our current knowledge or abilities, but still require some effort to answer.

The Power of Open Questions

Questions come in many forms, but one key distinction is between closed and open questions.

Closed questions have a limited set of possible answers. They often can be answered with a simple "yes" or "no" or a specific piece of information. For example:

"Is it raining outside?"

"What time is the meeting?"

"Do you prefer coffee or tea?"

Open questions, on the other hand, allow for a wide range of responses. They often start with words like "how," "why," or "what." For example:

"How do you feel about the new policy?"

"Why do you think the project failed?"

"What could we do to improve customer satisfaction?"

While closed questions are useful for getting specific information, open questions are powerful tools for stimulating thinking. They encourage people to reflect, analyze, and express their thoughts more fully.

When we're asked an open question, our brains have to work harder. We need to search our memories, make connections, and often come up with new ideas. This deeper level of processing helps us learn and remember better.

Open questions also give us more freedom in how we respond. This can lead to more creative and unexpected answers. Many great discoveries and innovations have come from asking open-ended questions that challenge assumptions and encourage new ways of thinking.

The Framing Effect

The way a question is asked can significantly influence how people answer it. This is known as the framing effect.

For example, imagine a doctor telling a patient about a surgery. If the doctor says, "The surgery has a 90% survival rate," the patient might feel more positive about it than if the doctor said, "The surgery has a 10% mortality rate." The information is the same, but the framing is different.

This effect applies to all kinds of questions. Consider these two ways of asking about a new product:

"What do you like about this product?"

"What problems do you see with this product?"

The first question frames the product positively and might lead to more favorable responses. The second frames it negatively and might encourage more critical feedback.

Being aware of framing can help us ask better questions. We can choose frames that encourage the kind of thinking we want to promote. At the same time, we should be careful not to use framing in ways that unfairly bias responses.

Questions and Emotion

Questions don't just affect our thoughts; they also influence our emotions. The right question at the right time can change how we feel about a situation.

For instance, when faced with a challenge, asking "What's the worst that could happen?" might increase anxiety. But asking "What's the best possible outcome?" could inspire hope and motivation.

Questions can also help us manage our emotions. Psychologists often use questions to help people examine and change their emotional responses. For example:

"What evidence do I have for this feeling?"

"How else could I look at this situation?"

"What would I tell a friend if they were in this situation?"

These kinds of questions can help us step back from our immediate emotional reactions and think more clearly.

The Power of Self-Questioning

We often think of questions as something we ask others, but some of the most powerful questions are the ones we ask ourselves. Self-questioning is a key part of metacognition – our ability to think about our own thinking.

Good self-questions can help us:

Set goals: "What do I really want to achieve?"

Solve problems: "What am I assuming that might not be true?"

Learn: "How can I apply this information to my life?"

Grow: "What can I learn from this experience?"

Research has shown that people who regularly engage in self-questioning tend to be better problem-solvers and learners. They're more aware of their own thought processes and better able to direct their thinking in productive ways.

However, self-questioning can also be harmful if done in an overly negative or critical way. Questions like "Why am I so stupid?" or "What's wrong with me?" can reinforce negative self-perceptions and lead to anxiety or depression.

The key is to use self-questions that are constructive and growth-oriented. Instead of "Why can't I do this?", try "How can I learn to do this better?"

Questions and Memory

Questions play a crucial role in how we remember information. When we're asked a question, we have to actively recall the answer. This process of retrieval strengthens the memory, making it easier to recall in the future.

This is why quizzes and tests can be such effective learning tools. They force us to retrieve information from our memory, reinforcing what we've learned.

But it's not just answering questions that helps memory. Asking questions about what we're learning can also improve recall. When we generate our own questions, we have to think deeply about the material and make connections to what we already know.

For example, if you're reading a history book, you might ask yourself:

"How does this event connect to what happened before?"

"What might have happened if things had gone differently?"

"How does this relate to events in the present day?"

These kinds of questions help us engage more actively with the material and form stronger, more lasting memories.

The Social Impact of Questions

Questions don't just affect individuals; they can shape entire conversations and relationships. The questions we ask (or don't ask) send powerful messages about what we value and how we see others.

Asking thoughtful questions shows that we're interested in others and value their thoughts and experiences. This can build trust and deepen relationships. On the flip side, always talking about ourselves without asking questions can make us seem self-centered and uninterested in others.

Questions can also change the dynamics of a group. In a meeting, for instance, asking "What does everyone think about this?" can encourage more participation and diverse viewpoints. Asking "Why don't we try a new approach?" can spark innovation and challenge the status quo.

However, questions can also be used in negative ways. Repeated questions can feel like an interrogation. Leading questions can manipulate people's responses. And some questions can be insulting or hurtful if they're based on false assumptions or stereotypes.

Being aware of how our questions affect others can help us communicate more effectively and build stronger relationships.

Questions and Critical Thinking

Questions are at the heart of critical thinking. They help us examine assumptions, evaluate evidence, and consider different perspectives.

Some key critical thinking questions include:

"What evidence supports this claim?"

"Are there other possible explanations?"

"What are the potential consequences of this action?"

"How reliable is this source of information?"

By habitually asking these kinds of questions, we can become more discerning thinkers. We're less likely to be fooled by false information or flawed arguments. We're better able to make informed decisions and solve complex problems.

However, critical thinking questions can sometimes be uncomfortable. They challenge our beliefs and force us to consider that we might be wrong. This is why some people avoid asking these kinds of questions – it's easier to stick with what we already believe.

Developing a habit of critical questioning takes practice and courage. It means being willing to challenge our own assumptions and being open to changing our minds when the evidence warrants it.

The Neuroscience of Questioning

Recent advances in neuroscience have given us new insights into how questions affect our brains. When we're asked a question, several things happen in our brain:

Attention activation: Questions activate our brain's attention networks. They signal that there's something important to focus on.

Memory search: Our brain starts searching through our memories for relevant information.

Emotional engagement: Questions can trigger emotional responses, activating areas of the brain involved in emotion and motivation.

Cognitive processing: As we consider the question and possible answers, areas of the brain involved in reasoning and decision-making become active.

Reward anticipation: If we think we might know the answer, our brain's reward system gets activated, creating a sense of anticipation.

This complex brain activity explains why questions can be so engaging and why they're such powerful tools for learning and problem-solving.

Questions are far more than simple requests for information. They're powerful tools that shape how we think, feel, and interact with the world. By understanding the psychology behind questions, we can use them more effectively in all areas of our lives.

Salient points:

Our brains are naturally curious and respond positively to well-crafted questions.

Open questions encourage deeper thinking and more creative responses.

The way we frame questions can significantly influence the answers we get.

Questions affect our emotions as well as our thoughts.

Self-questioning is a powerful tool for personal growth and learning.

Questions play a crucial role in memory and learning.

The questions we ask (or don't ask) have a big impact on our relationships and social interactions.

Critical thinking questions help us make better decisions and solve problems more effectively.

As we move forward, keep these psychological insights in mind. They'll help you craft better questions and use them more effectively in all areas of your life. In the next chapter, we'll look at specific techniques for asking powerful questions.

# Types of Questions

Questions come in many forms, each with its own purpose and effect. Understanding these different types can help you choose the right question for any situation. In this chapter, we'll explore three main categories of questions: open versus closed questions, probing questions, and leading questions.

Open vs. Closed Questions

The most basic way to classify questions is as either open or closed. This distinction is crucial because it greatly affects the kind of answer you're likely to get.

Closed Questions

Closed questions are those that can be answered with a simple "yes" or "no," or with a specific piece of information. They're straightforward and usually have only one correct answer. For example:

"Are you hungry?"

"What time is it?"

"Did you finish your homework?"

"How old are you?"

Closed questions are useful when you need specific information quickly. They're great for:

Confirming facts: "Is this report due on Friday?"

Making decisions: "Should we go to the movies or stay home?"

Getting clear answers: "Did you understand the instructions?"

However, closed questions have limitations. They don't encourage detailed responses or deeper thinking. If you only ask closed questions, you might miss out on valuable information and insights.

Open Questions

Open questions, on the other hand, invite longer, more thoughtful answers. They often start with words like "how," "why," or "what." Open questions don't have a single correct answer. Instead, they encourage the person to share their thoughts, feelings, or opinions. For example:

"How did you feel about the movie?"

"What do you think caused the problem?"

"Why did you choose this career?"

"How could we improve this process?"

Open questions are powerful tools for:

Starting conversations: "What's on your mind today?"

Gathering opinions: "What do you think about this new policy?"

Encouraging reflection: "How might you handle this situation differently next time?"

Sparking creativity: "What could we do to make this project more exciting?"

Open questions can lead to surprising and insightful answers. They show that you're interested in the other person's thoughts and are willing to listen. However, open questions can also be time-consuming and might not be suitable when you need a quick, specific answer.

Choosing Between Open and Closed Questions

Knowing when to use open or closed questions is a key skill. Here are some guidelines:

Use closed questions when:

You need specific information quickly

You're clarifying something

You're trying to focus a conversation that has gone off track

Use open questions when:

You want to explore a topic in depth

You're trying to understand someone's feelings or opinions

You want to encourage creative thinking

You're starting a conversation or trying to build rapport

Often, the best approach is to use a mix of both types. You might start with an open question to get a broad view, then use closed questions to fill in specific details.

Probing Questions

Probing questions are follow-up questions that dig deeper into a topic. They're used to get more information, clarify understanding, or explore ideas further. Probing questions are especially useful when the initial answer is vague or incomplete.

Here are some examples of probing questions:

"Can you tell me more about that?"

"What do you mean by...?"

"How did that make you feel?"

"What happened next?"

"Can you give me an example?"

Probing questions are valuable tools for:

Getting details: When someone gives a general answer, probing questions can uncover specific information.

Understanding emotions: Probing can help you understand not just what happened, but how someone felt about it.

Exploring ideas: When brainstorming or problem-solving, probing questions can help develop initial ideas further.

Checking understanding: If you're not sure you've understood correctly, probing questions can help clarify.

Here's an example of how probing questions might work in a conversation:

Initial question: "How was your vacation?" Initial answer: "It was good." Probing questions:

"What was your favorite part of the trip?"

"Did anything unexpected happen?"

"How did this vacation compare to others you've taken?"

By using probing questions, you can turn a simple exchange into a more meaningful conversation.

Tips for Using Probing Questions

Listen carefully: Pay attention to the initial answer so you can ask relevant follow-up questions.

Be genuinely curious: Your interest will encourage the other person to share more.

Use open-ended probes: Questions that start with "how" or "what" often lead to more detailed responses.

Be patient: Give the person time to think and respond.

Watch your tone: Make sure your questions sound interested, not like an interrogation.

Know when to stop: If the person seems uncomfortable or has clearly shared all they want to, it's time to move on.

Leading Questions

Leading questions are questions that push the respondent towards a particular answer. They often contain assumptions or suggest a desired response. For example:

"Don't you think this is the best solution?"

"Isn't it true that you were late to work yesterday?"

"You like chocolate ice cream, right?"

Leading questions can be problematic because they can influence the answer. They might make people agree with something they don't really believe, or prevent them from sharing their true thoughts.

However, leading questions aren't always bad. They can be useful in certain situations:

Confirming agreement: "We're all on board with this plan, aren't we?"

Offering reassurance: "You're feeling better now, right?"

In sales: "Wouldn't you love to have this product in your home?"

In courtroom settings: Lawyers sometimes use leading questions to guide witness testimony.

The key is to be aware of when you're using leading questions and to consider whether they're appropriate for your goals.

Avoiding Unintentional Leading Questions

Sometimes we ask leading questions without realizing it. Here are some tips to avoid this:

Be aware of your own biases: Try to ask questions that don't reflect your personal opinions.

Use neutral language: Avoid words that suggest a "right" answer.

Ask open-ended questions: These allow people to answer in their own words.

Offer multiple options: Instead of "Do you agree?", try "Do you agree, disagree, or have a different view?"

Be careful with your tone: Even a neutral question can become leading if said with the right inflection.

Comparing Question Types

To better understand these different types of questions, let's look at how they might be used in a specific situation. Imagine you're a manager trying to understand why a project is behind schedule.

Closed question: "Is the project delayed?" This gets a quick yes or no answer but doesn't provide any details about why.

Open question: "What factors have affected the project timeline?" This invites a more detailed response and might reveal issues you hadn't considered.

Probing question: (After hearing about one factor) "How has that specifically impacted our deadlines?" This digs deeper into the information provided, helping you understand the full impact of the issue.

Leading question: "The delay is because of the software issues, right?" This suggests a cause for the delay, which might prevent other factors from being mentioned.

Each type of question has its place, and skilled questioners know how to use them all effectively.

Practical Exercise: Improving Your Questioning Skills

To help you practice using different types of questions, try this exercise:

Choose a topic you want to learn more about. It could be a hobby, a current event, or something about a friend or family member.

Write down:

- 3 closed questions about the topic

- 3 open questions

- 3 probing questions that could follow up on the open questions

- 1 leading question (and then rewrite it as a non-leading question)

If possible, ask these questions to someone knowledgeable about the topic. Notice how different types of questions lead to different kinds of answers.

Reflect on which questions were most effective in helping you learn about the topic.

Becoming skilled at asking good questions takes practice. Pay attention to the questions you ask in your daily life. Are they mostly open or closed? Do you use probing questions when you want more information? Do you sometimes ask leading questions without meaning to?

As you become more aware of the types of questions you ask, you'll naturally start to choose the right type of question for each situation. Over time, you'll find that your conversations become richer, your understanding deepens, and your ability to solve problems improves.

## Author Profile

# Crafting the Perfect Question

Dr. A.P.J. Abdul Kalam, known as the "Missile Man of India," was not just a brilliant scientist but also a master of asking the right questions. His curiosity and questioning nature played a crucial role in his journey from a humble background to becoming one of India's most respected figures.

One particular incident stands out. In the late 1970s, Dr. Kalam was working on India's first satellite launch vehicle, SLV-3. The project faced numerous setbacks, including a failed launch in August 1979 that left the team demoralized.

Instead of giving up or blindly pushing forward, Dr. Kalam took a different approach. He gathered his team and asked a series of probing questions:

"What exactly went wrong?" "Why did our calculations fail?" "What are we missing?" "How can we prevent this from happening again?"

These questions weren't accusatory or negative. Instead, they encouraged the team to think deeply and critically about the problem. Dr. Kalam created an environment where people felt safe to share their thoughts and ideas.

As the team worked through these questions, they uncovered a small but critical error in their calculations. This discovery led to modifications in the design and, eventually, to a successful launch in July 1980.

Dr. Kalam's questioning didn't stop there. He continually asked, "What's next? How can we do better?" This forward-thinking approach drove India's space program to new heights.

Crafting good questions is a skill that can be learned and improved with practice. Two key aspects of crafting effective questions: clarity and precision, and contextual relevance. By mastering these elements, you'll be able to ask questions that lead to more insightful answers and meaningful conversations.

Clarity and Precision

Clear and precise questions are the foundation of productive inquiry. When you ask a question that is easy to understand and specific in its intent, you're more likely to receive a helpful and accurate response. Let's explore some techniques for improving the clarity and precision of your questions:

Use simple language: Avoid complex words or jargon that might confuse your audience. Choose words that are easily understood by the person you're asking. For example, instead of saying "What is the optimal methodology for completing this task?" you could ask "What's the best way to do this?"

Be specific: Vague questions often lead to vague answers. Narrow down your query to focus on the exact information you need. For instance, rather than asking "How's the weather?" you could ask "What's the temperature outside right now?"

Avoid ambiguity: Make sure your question can't be interpreted in multiple ways. If there's potential for misunderstanding, rephrase the question to eliminate any confusion. For example, instead of asking "When did you go to the store?" you could ask "What time did you go to the grocery store today?"

Use concrete terms: Abstract concepts can be difficult to grasp. Whenever possible, use tangible examples or specific scenarios to make your question more concrete. For instance, instead of asking "How can I improve my communication skills?" you could ask "What are three specific things I can do to communicate more effectively in team meetings?"

Break down complex questions: If you find yourself asking a question that covers multiple points, consider breaking it into smaller, more manageable questions. This approach makes it easier for the person answering to provide thorough responses to each part.

Be concise: While it's important to provide context, avoid unnecessarily long or wordy questions. Trim any excess information that doesn't directly contribute to the core of your inquiry.

Use appropriate qualifiers: When necessary, include qualifiers to make your question more precise. For example, instead of asking "How many people live in

New York?" you could ask "What is the estimated population of New York City as of the most recent census?"

Avoid leading questions: Make sure your questions don't suggest a preferred answer. Leading questions can bias the response and limit the information you receive. For instance, instead of asking "Don't you think this new policy is unfair?" you could ask "What are your thoughts on the new policy?"

Contextual Relevance

Questions that are relevant to the context in which they're asked are more likely to yield useful answers. Consider the following points to ensure your questions are contextually appropriate:

Understand the situation: Before asking a question, take a moment to assess the current circumstances. Consider factors such as the setting, the people involved, and any relevant background information. This understanding will help you frame your question in a way that fits the context.

Consider timing: Ask your question at an appropriate moment. For example, a detailed question about a project might be better asked during a scheduled meeting rather than in a casual hallway conversation.

Tailor your question to the audience: Different people have different levels of knowledge and experience. Adjust your question based on who you're asking. A question you'd ask an expert might be very different from one you'd ask a beginner.

Build on previous information: If you're in an ongoing conversation or learning process, use what you've already learned to inform your next question. This shows that you're engaged and helps to create a logical flow of information.

Be mindful of cultural context: In diverse settings, be aware of cultural differences that might affect how your question is perceived or answered. What's appropriate in one culture might be considered impolite or irrelevant in another.

Align with goals: Ensure your question supports the overall objective of the conversation or task at hand.

Ask yourself, "How does this question help us move forward or gain necessary information?"

Consider the scope: Make sure your question is neither too broad nor too narrow for the given context. A question that's too broad might lead to vague or overwhelming responses, while one that's too narrow might miss important related information.

Be aware of sensitive topics: In some contexts, certain questions might be inappropriate or uncomfortable. Use your judgment to determine if a question is suitable for the situation.

Provide necessary background: If your question requires some context to be understood, provide a brief explanation before asking. This helps the person answering to give a more informed and relevant response.

Follow up appropriately: Based on the answer you receive, be prepared to ask follow-up questions that dig deeper or clarify points. This shows that you're actively listening and engaged in the conversation.

By focusing on clarity, precision, and contextual relevance, you can significantly improve the quality of your questions. Remember that asking good questions is a skill that develops over time. Pay attention to how others respond to your questions and be willing to refine your approach based on what you learn.

As you practice these techniques, you'll find that your questions become more effective tools for gathering information, stimulating discussion, and promoting understanding. Well-crafted questions can open doors to new insights, foster meaningful conversations, and drive personal and professional growth.

# Asking the Right Questions

In our quest to become better questioners, we must learn how to ask the right questions. This skill is crucial for getting the information we need and steering conversations in productive directions. In this chapter, we'll explore two key aspects of asking the right questions: identifying objectives and aligning questions with goals.

Identifying Objectives

Before we can ask the right questions, we need to know what we're trying to achieve. Identifying our objectives is the first step in this process. Here's how to do it:

Define your purpose: Start by asking yourself why you're seeking information. Are you trying to solve a problem, make a decision, or learn something new? Having a clear purpose will guide your questioning process.

Example: If you're interviewing a job candidate, your purpose might be to determine if they're a good fit for the position.

Outline your desired outcomes: What specific information or results do you hope to gain from your questions? Make a list of the key points you want to address.

Example: For a job interview, your desired outcomes might include:

Understanding the candidate's relevant experience:

Assessing their problem-solving skills

Evaluating their fit with the company culture

Consider the context: Think about the situation in which you'll be asking questions. Who is your audience? What is their background and level of expertise? What constraints or limitations might you face?

Example: If you're interviewing a senior executive, you'll need to tailor your questions to their level of experience and the specific challenges of the role.

Prioritize your objectives: Not all objectives are equally important. Rank your goals in order of priority to ensure you focus on the most critical aspects first.

Example: In a job interview, assessing the candidate's relevant skills might be more important than discussing their long-term career goals.

Be flexible: While it's important to have clear objectives, be prepared to adjust them as new information comes to light. Sometimes, unexpected insights can lead to valuable new lines of inquiry.

Aligning Questions with Goals

Once you've identified your objectives, the next step is to craft questions that will help you achieve those goals. Here's how to align your questions with your objectives:

Use different types of questions: There are various types of questions, each suited for different purposes. Some common types include:

Open-ended questions: These encourage detailed responses and are useful for gathering in-depth information. Example: "Can you describe a challenging project you've worked on?"

Closed-ended questions: These typically require a yes/no or short answer and are good for confirming specific details. Example: "Do you have experience with Python programming?"

Probing questions: These follow up on previous answers to get more information or clarification. Example: "You mentioned leading a team. How many people did you manage?"

Hypothetical questions: These present imaginary scenarios to assess problem-solving skills or thought processes. Example: "How would you handle a situation where a team member consistently misses deadlines?"

Choose the type of question that best fits your objective for each piece of information you're seeking.

Start broad, then narrow down Begin with general questions to get an overview, then use more specific questions to focus on the details that matter most to your objectives.

Example: Broad: "Tell me about your experience in marketing." Narrow: "What specific strategies did you use to increase social media engagement in your last role?"

Use clear and concise language: Phrase your questions in a way that's easy to understand. Avoid jargon or complex language unless you're sure the other person is familiar with it.

Example: Instead of asking, "What methodologies did you employ to optimize customer acquisition?" try "How did you attract new customers?"

Avoid leading questions: Make sure your questions don't suggest a preferred answer. This can bias the responses you receive and lead to inaccurate information.

Example: Instead of asking, "Don't you think our product is the best on the market?" try "How does our product compare to others you've used?"

Ask one thing at a time: Avoid compound questions that ask multiple things at once. These can be confusing and may result in incomplete answers.

Example: Instead of asking, "What's your educational background, work experience, and why do you want this job?" break it into separate questions.

Use follow-up questions: Prepare follow-up questions to dig deeper into important topics. This shows you're actively listening and helps you gather more detailed information.

Example: If someone mentions a successful project, you might ask, "What specific challenges did you face, and how did you overcome them?"

Tailor questions to your audience: Consider the background and expertise of the person you're questioning. Adjust your language and the complexity of your questions accordingly.

Example: When talking to a technical expert, you might use more specialized terminology than when discussing the same topic with a general audience.

Test your questions: Before using your questions in an important situation, try them out on a colleague or friend. This can help you identify any unclear or ineffective questions.

Be prepared to adapt While it's good to have a list of prepared questions, be ready to adjust your approach based on the answers you receive. Sometimes, unexpected information can lead to new and valuable lines of inquiry.

Reflect on your questioning strategy: After each questioning session, take some time to evaluate how well your questions aligned with your objectives. Did you get the information you needed? Were there any areas where your questions fell short? Use these insights to improve your questioning skills for next time.

By carefully identifying your objectives and aligning your questions with those goals, you'll be better equipped to ask the right questions in any situation. This approach will help you gather more relevant and useful information, leading to better decisions and more productive conversations.

Asking the right questions is a skill that improves with practice. As you apply these techniques in various situations, you'll become more adept at crafting questions that get to the heart of what you need to know. Keep refining your approach, and you'll find that your ability to ask effective questions becomes a powerful tool in both your personal and professional life.

# Questioning Techniques for Different Situations

Asking the right questions in various contexts can lead to better understanding, improved relationships, and more effective problem-solving. This chapter explores questioning techniques for personal conversations, professional settings, and investigative scenarios.

In Personal Conversations

Open-ended questions

Open-ended questions encourage detailed responses and promote deeper conversations. Instead of asking "Did you have a good day?", try "What happened during your day?" This allows the other person to share more information and express their thoughts and feelings.

Examples:

"How do you feel about...?"

"What are your thoughts on...?"

"Can you tell me more about...?"

Reflective questions

Reflective questions show that you're listening and help clarify what the other person is saying. They often involve repeating or rephrasing part of what was said.

Examples:

"So, you're saying that...?"

"It sounds like you feel... Is that right?"

"If I understand correctly, you think..."

Empathetic questions

These questions show that you care about the other person's feelings and experiences. They help build emotional connections and trust.

Examples:

"How did that make you feel?"

"What was that experience like for you?"

"What do you need right now?"

Hypothetical questions

Hypothetical questions can help explore different perspectives and possibilities. They can also be useful for discussing sensitive topics indirectly.

Examples:

"If you could change one thing about the situation, what would it be?"

"How would you handle it if...?"

"What would you do differently if you could go back in time?"

Clarifying questions

These questions help you understand unclear or ambiguous information. They show that you're paying attention and want to grasp the full picture.

Examples:

"Could you explain what you mean by...?"

"When you say..., do you mean...?"

"Can you give me an example of that?"

In Professional Settings

Goal-oriented questions

These questions focus on objectives, outcomes, and results. They help keep discussions on track and solution-focused.

Examples:

"What are we trying to achieve here?"

"How will we measure success in this project?"

"What specific outcomes are we aiming for?"

Problem-solving questions

These questions help identify issues and find solutions. They encourage creative thinking and collaboration.

Examples:

"What obstacles are we facing?"

"How have similar problems been solved in the past?"

"What resources do we need to overcome this challenge?"

Decision-making questions

These questions help gather information and opinions to make informed decisions. They can also help build consensus among team members.

Examples:

"What are the pros and cons of each option?"

"How does this align with our long-term goals?"

"What potential risks should we consider?"

Performance-related questions

These questions are useful for evaluating work, giving feedback, and setting expectations.

Examples:

"How do you think you performed on this task?"

"What support do you need to improve in this area?"

"How can we make this process more efficient?"

Stakeholder questions

These questions help understand the needs and perspectives of various stakeholders in a project or decision.

Examples:

"How will this impact our customers/clients?"

"What concerns might other departments have about this?"

"Who else should we involve in this discussion?"

Strategic questions

These questions focus on long-term planning, vision, and organizational direction.

Examples:

"How does this fit into our overall strategy?"

"What trends in our industry should we be preparing for?"

"Where do we want to be in five years, and how do we get there?"

In Investigative Scenarios

Fact-gathering questions

These questions aim to collect basic information and establish a foundation for further inquiry.

Examples:

"What happened?"

"When and where did this occur?"

"Who was involved?"

Sequencing questions

These questions help establish the order of events and identify any gaps in the timeline.

Examples:

"What happened next?"

"Can you walk me through the events in order?"

"When did you first notice...?"

Comparative questions

These questions help identify similarities, differences, and patterns.

Examples:

"How does this compare to previous incidents?"

"Have you noticed any similar occurrences?"

"What's different about this situation?"

Probing questions

These questions dig deeper into specific details or areas of interest. They often follow up on previous responses.

Examples:

"Can you elaborate on that point?"

"Why do you think that happened?"

"What makes you say that?"

Behavior-focused questions

These questions explore actions, reactions, and decision-making processes.

Examples:

"What did you do when you saw...?"

"How did others react to...?"

"Why did you choose to...?"

Corroborative questions

These questions help verify information and identify potential sources of evidence.

Examples:

"Who else was present when this happened?"

"Are there any records or documents that support this?"

"Can anyone else confirm what you've told me?"

Hypothetical scenario questions

These questions can help explore alternative explanations or test the credibility of a statement.

Examples:

"If someone else had been in your position, what might they have done?"

"What would have happened if...?"

"Can you think of any reason why someone might have...?"

Tips for Effective Questioning Across All Situations

Listen actively: Pay close attention to responses and use them to guide your next questions.

Use silence: Allow pauses after asking questions to give the other person time to think and respond fully.

Avoid leading questions: Don't phrase questions in a way that suggests a particular answer.

Be neutral: Keep your tone and body language non-judgmental to encourage open and honest responses.

Ask one question at a time: Avoid overwhelming the other person with multiple questions at once.

Be flexible: Be ready to adjust your questioning strategy based on the responses you receive.

Practice empathy: Try to understand the other person's perspective and feelings throughout the conversation.

Follow up: Use the information you gather to ask more specific, relevant questions as the conversation progresses.

By mastering these questioning techniques and applying them appropriately in different situations, you can become a more effective communicator, problem-solver, and investigator. Remember that the art of questioning is not just about asking the right questions, but also about creating an environment where others feel comfortable sharing information and insights.

# Exploring Assumptions

Assumptions play a crucial role in our thinking and decision-making processes. They are the unspoken beliefs and ideas that we take for granted, often without realizing it. In this chapter, we'll examine how to spot these hidden assumptions and learn techniques to question and clarify them effectively.

Identifying Hidden Assumptions

Hidden assumptions are like invisible foundations that support our thoughts and actions. They're often so deeply ingrained that we don't even notice them. However, recognizing these assumptions is the first step in improving our critical thinking and decision-making skills.

Here are some strategies to help you spot hidden assumptions:

Look for unstated premises: When examining an argument or statement, try to identify any underlying beliefs that aren't explicitly mentioned but are necessary for the conclusion to be true.

Question the obvious: Sometimes, the most apparent things are the ones we overlook. Ask yourself, "What am I taking for granted here?"

Consider alternative perspectives: Try to view the situation from different angles. This can help reveal assumptions that might be specific to your own point of view.

Examine your emotional reactions: Strong emotional responses often indicate underlying assumptions. If you feel strongly about something, ask yourself why.

Pay attention to language: Certain words and phrases can hint at hidden assumptions. For example, using "obviously" or "everyone knows" might signal an unexamined belief.

Look for generalizations: Broad statements often hide assumptions about entire groups or categories.

Identify cultural influences: Our cultural background shapes many of our assumptions. Be aware of how your cultural context might influence your thinking.

Consider historical context: Many assumptions are rooted in past experiences or societal norms.

Understanding the historical background can help uncover these.

Analyze analogies and metaphors: These linguistic tools often carry hidden assumptions about how different concepts relate to each other.

Examine your decision-making process: When making choices, pause to consider what assumptions are guiding your decisions.

Example: Let's say someone argues, "We need to increase police funding to reduce crime rates."

Hidden assumptions might include:

More police funding leads to less crime

The current crime rate is too high

Police are effective at preventing crime

There aren't other, more effective ways to reduce crime

By identifying these assumptions, we can begin to question and examine them more closely.

Challenging and Clarifying Assumptions

Once you've identified hidden assumptions, the next step is to challenge and clarify them. This process helps refine your thinking and leads to more robust conclusions.

Here are some techniques for challenging and clarifying assumptions:

Ask probing questions: Use open-ended questions to dig deeper into the reasoning behind an assumption. For example, "What evidence supports this belief?" or "How did you come to this conclusion?"

Seek evidence: Look for data or research that either supports or contradicts the assumption. Be open to information that challenges your existing beliefs.

Consider counterexamples: Try to think of situations where the assumption doesn't hold true. This can help reveal the limits of its applicability.

Use the "Five Whys" technique: Keep asking "Why?" to get to the root of an assumption. Often, the fifth "why" reveals the core belief or assumption.

Play devil's advocate: Argue against your own assumptions or those of others. This can help reveal weaknesses in the reasoning.

Consult diverse sources: Seek out information and opinions from a variety of perspectives to challenge your assumptions.

Test the assumption: If possible, design an experiment or find a way to test the assumption in a real-world context.

Analyze potential consequences: Think through what would happen if the assumption were false. This can help you assess its importance and validity.

Break down complex assumptions: Some assumptions are actually combinations of several smaller assumptions. Try to separate these for individual examination.

Use conditional statements: Rephrase assumptions using "if-then" statements to clarify their logical structure.

Consider alternative explanations: Try to come up with other possible explanations for the observed phenomena that don't rely on the assumption.

Examine the source: Consider where the assumption came from. Is it based on personal experience, hearsay, or reliable research?

Example: Let's return to the assumption "More police funding leads to less crime."

To challenge and clarify this assumption, we might:

Ask: "What evidence supports the link between police funding and crime rates?"

Look for studies on the relationship between police funding and crime rates

Consider places where increased police funding didn't reduce crime

Examine alternative factors that might influence crime rates (e.g., economic conditions, education, social programs)

Test the assumption by comparing crime rates in areas with different levels of police funding

Analyze potential unintended consequences of increased police funding

By going through this process, we can develop a more nuanced understanding of the relationship between police funding and crime rates, rather than relying on a simplified assumption.

The Importance of Exploring Assumptions

Examining assumptions is a vital skill for several reasons:

Improved critical thinking: By questioning assumptions, you develop a more analytical and thoughtful approach to information and ideas.

Better decision-making: Understanding the assumptions behind your choices helps you make more informed and effective decisions.

Enhanced communication: Recognizing and clarifying assumptions can lead to clearer and more productive discussions with others.

Increased creativity: Challenging assumptions often leads to new ideas and innovative solutions.

Greater empathy: Understanding the assumptions of others can help you better appreciate different perspectives and experiences.

Reduced bias: Many of our biases are rooted in unexamined assumptions. By exploring these, we can work to minimize their impact.

More accurate predictions: Assumptions often underlie our expectations about the future. Examining them can lead to more accurate forecasting.

Improved problem-solving: Many problems persist because of hidden assumptions. Identifying and challenging these can lead to breakthrough solutions.

Conclusion

Exploring assumptions is a powerful tool for improving our thinking and decision-making. By learning to identify hidden assumptions and developing techniques to challenge and clarify them, we can gain a deeper understanding of complex issues and make more informed choices.

The goal isn't to eliminate all assumptions — that's neither possible nor desirable. Instead, the aim is to become more aware of our assumptions and to examine them critically when necessary. This process of questioning and clarification leads to more robust thinking and better outcomes in both personal and professional contexts.

As you continue to practice these skills, you'll find that exploring assumptions becomes a natural part of your thought process, enhancing your ability to navigate complex ideas and make sound decisions in an increasingly complex world.

# Questioning for Problem Solving

Problem solving is a vital skill in both personal and professional life. By asking the right questions, we can better understand issues, find their sources, and create effective solutions. This chapter focuses on two key aspects of questioning for problem solving: root cause analysis and creative problem-solving techniques.

Root Cause Analysis

Root cause analysis is a method used to identify the fundamental reason behind a problem, rather than just addressing its symptoms. By asking a series of probing questions, we can dig deeper into an issue and uncover its true origin. Here are some effective questioning strategies for root cause analysis:

The "5 Whys" technique: This simple but powerful method involves asking "Why?" five times in succession, each time building on the previous answer. For example:

Problem: The car won't start. Why? The battery is dead. Why? The alternator isn't working. Why? The alternator belt has broken. Why? The belt was old and hadn't been replaced. Why? Regular maintenance checks were not performed.

By the fifth "why," we've identified the root cause: lack of regular maintenance. This insight allows us to address the real issue and prevent similar problems in the future.

Fishbone diagram questions: Also known as the Ishikawa diagram, this tool helps visualize potential causes of a problem. Start by stating the main problem, then ask questions about different categories that might contribute to it, such as:

People: Who is involved? What are their roles?

Process: What steps led to the problem? Where did the issue first appear?

Equipment: What tools or machinery are involved? Are they functioning correctly?

Materials: What resources are used? Are they of good quality?

Environment: What external factors might be influencing the situation?

Is/Is Not analysis: This method helps clarify the problem by asking what it is and what it isn't. Questions might include:

Where does the problem occur? Where doesn't it occur?

When does it happen? When doesn't it happen?

Who experiences the problem? Who doesn't experience it?

What specific products or processes are affected? Which aren't affected?

By contrasting what is and isn't part of the problem, we can narrow down potential causes and focus our investigation more effectively.

Change analysis: When a problem suddenly appears, it's often due to a recent change. Ask questions like:

What has changed recently in our processes, materials, or environment?

When did we first notice the problem?

What happened just before the issue arose?

Have there been any personnel changes that might be relevant?

These questions can help pinpoint what triggered the problem and guide us toward a solution.

Creative Problem-Solving Techniques

Once we've identified the root cause of a problem, we need to generate potential solutions. Creative problem-solving techniques use questioning to spark innovative ideas and approach issues from new angles. Here are some effective methods:

SCAMPER technique: SCAMPER is an acronym that stands for Substitute, Combine, Adapt, Modify, Put to another use, Eliminate, and Reverse. For each of these actions, ask questions like:

Substitute: What can we use instead? Who else could do this?

Combine: How can we merge this with other ideas or processes?

Adapt: How can we adjust this to work in a different context?

Modify: How can we change the shape, color, or size?

Put to another use: What else could this be used for?

Eliminate: What can we remove or simplify?

Reverse: What if we did this backwards or in a different order?

Random word association: Choose a random word and ask how it relates to your problem. For example, if your problem is "How to increase sales" and your random word is "tree," you might ask:

How can we "branch out" to new markets?

How can we make our product line grow like a tree?

What if we used a tree-like structure for our sales team?

This technique forces your brain to make unexpected connections, often leading to creative solutions.

Reverse thinking: Instead of asking how to solve a problem, ask how to make it worse. Then, reverse those ideas. For example:

Problem: How to reduce customer complaints Reverse: How to increase customer complaints Ideas:

Ignore customer feedback

Deliver products late

Make the return process complicated

Now, reverse these ideas:

Actively seek and respond to customer feedback

Improve delivery times

Simplify the return process

This method can help you see the problem from a new perspective and generate ideas you might not have considered otherwise.

Role-playing questions: Imagine different people or entities facing your problem and ask what they would do. For example:

What would a child do in this situation?

How would a competitor handle this?

What approach would a completely different industry take?

These questions can lead to fresh, unexpected solutions by forcing you to step outside your usual thinking patterns.

Future scenario questions: Project yourself into the future and ask questions as if the problem has already been solved:

How did we overcome this challenge?

What key changes did we make?

What new skills or resources did we need to develop?

This technique can help you visualize potential solutions and the steps needed to achieve them.

Analogy questions: Look for similar problems in other fields and ask how they were solved. For example:

How do other industries handle similar issues?

Can we find a parallel problem in nature? How is it resolved?

What if this problem were a physical object? How would we fix it?

By drawing parallels with unrelated areas, you can gain new insights and ideas for your own problem.

Conclusion

Effective questioning is a powerful tool for problem solving. By using root cause analysis techniques, we can identify the true source of issues rather than just treating symptoms. Creative problem-solving methods then allow us to generate innovative solutions by approaching problems from new angles.

Remember, the key to successful problem solving through questioning is to remain curious and open-minded. Don't be afraid to ask "silly" questions or explore seemingly unrelated ideas. Often, the most effective solutions come from unexpected places.

As you practice these techniques, you'll find that your problem-solving skills improve, allowing you to tackle complex issues more effectively. Keep refining your questioning skills, and you'll be better equipped to handle whatever challenges come your way.

# Eliciting Deep Insights

In our quest for knowledge and understanding, asking the right questions is only half the battle. The true art lies in drawing out meaningful, reflective responses that reveal hidden information and lead to profound insights. This chapter explores techniques to uncover deeper layers of understanding and encourage thoughtful, introspective answers.

Techniques for Uncovering Hidden Information

Active Listening

Active listening is a powerful tool for uncovering hidden information. By giving your full attention to the speaker and showing genuine interest, you create an environment where people feel comfortable sharing more than just surface-level information.

Key aspects of active listening include:

Maintaining eye contact

Using nonverbal cues like nodding to show engagement

Avoiding interruptions

Paraphrasing to confirm understanding

When people feel heard and understood, they're more likely to open up and share deeper thoughts and feelings.

## Follow-up Questions

Don't be satisfied with initial responses. Use follow-up questions to dig deeper and explore different angles of a topic. For example:

"Can you tell me more about that?"

"What makes you say that?"

"How did you come to that conclusion?"

These questions show that you're interested in understanding the full picture and can lead to unexpected revelations.

## Silence as a Tool

Many people feel uncomfortable with silence and rush to fill it. By allowing pauses in conversation, you give the other person time to think and potentially share more information. Count to five silently after someone finishes speaking before asking your next question. You might be surprised by what emerges in those moments of reflection.

Hypothetical Scenarios

Presenting hypothetical situations can help people think about issues from new angles and reveal hidden beliefs or motivations. For example:

"If you had unlimited resources, how would you approach this problem differently?"

This technique allows people to think beyond current constraints and can lead to innovative ideas and insights.

Reframing Questions

Sometimes, rephrasing a question can lead to new insights. If you're not getting the information you need, try asking the same question in a different way. For instance:

Instead of "What do you think about this project?", try "If you were in charge of this project, what would you do differently?"

Indirect Questions

Direct questions can sometimes make people feel defensive or put on the spot. Indirect questions can be less threatening and may lead to more honest, thoughtful responses. For example:

Instead of "Do you trust your coworkers?", try "How would you describe the level of trust in your team?"

Encouraging Reflective Responses

Open-ended Questions

Use questions that can't be answered with a simple "yes" or "no." Open-ended questions encourage people to think more deeply and provide detailed responses. For example:

"How did you feel when that happened?" "What factors influenced your decision?"

Asking "Why" (Carefully)

The question "Why?" can be a powerful tool for uncovering deeper motivations and reasoning. However, it's important to use it judiciously, as repeated "why" questions can feel accusatory or make people defensive. Instead, try variations like:

"What led you to that conclusion?" "Can you help me understand your reasoning?"

Encouraging Self-reflection

Ask questions that prompt people to examine their own thoughts, feelings, and behaviors. For example:

"Looking back, what would you do differently?" "How has this experience changed your perspective?"

These types of questions can lead to valuable insights and personal growth.

Using Analogies

Asking people to draw analogies can help them explain complex ideas or feelings in a more relatable way. For example:

"If this project were an animal, what would it be and why?"

This technique can lead to creative thinking and reveal underlying perceptions or emotions.

Scale Questions

Asking people to rate their experiences or feelings on a scale can provide a starting point for deeper discussion. For example:

"On a scale of 1 to 10, how satisfied are you with the outcome? Can you explain why you chose that number?"

Future-oriented Questions

Questions about the future can encourage people to think beyond their current situation and consider long-term implications or goals. For example:

"Where do you see this project in five years?" "How do you think this decision will affect future generations?"

Challenging Assumptions

Gently questioning assumptions can lead to new insights and encourage critical thinking. For example:

"What evidence supports that belief?" "Have you considered alternative explanations?"

Be careful to phrase these questions in a non-confrontational way to avoid defensiveness.

Encouraging Story-telling

Asking for specific examples or stories can lead to rich, detailed responses that reveal more than direct questions. For example:

"Can you tell me about a time when you faced a similar challenge?" "What's a memorable experience you've had related to this topic?"

Reflecting Feelings

Acknowledging and asking about emotions can lead to deeper, more personal insights. For example:

"It sounds like this was a frustrating experience for you. How did that affect your approach to the problem?"

Exploring Context

Questions that explore the broader context of a situation can reveal important factors that might otherwise be overlooked. For example:

"How does this issue relate to other challenges in your organization?" "What external factors might be influencing this situation?"

Conclusion

Eliciting deep insights is a skill that requires practice, patience, and genuine curiosity. By using these techniques, you can create an environment where people feel comfortable sharing their thoughts and feelings openly. Remember, the goal is not just to gather information, but to foster understanding and promote thoughtful reflection.

As you apply these techniques, be mindful of the other person's comfort level and respect their boundaries. Not everyone will be ready or willing to share deep insights immediately. Building trust and rapport over time can lead to more open and insightful conversations.

Finally, remember that eliciting deep insights is not just about asking the right questions, but also about truly listening to and valuing the responses you receive. By showing genuine interest and respect for others' perspectives, you create opportunities for meaningful dialogue and mutual learning.

# Leading Through Questions

Leaders often believe their role is to have all the answers. However, the most effective leaders know that asking the right questions is more powerful than always providing solutions. By using questions skillfully, leaders can guide their teams, encourage critical thinking, and create an environment where everyone contributes to problem-solving and innovation.

Why Questions Matter in Leadership

Questions are essential tools for leaders for several reasons:

They promote learning and growth: By asking questions, leaders show that it's okay not to know everything. This encourages a culture of continuous learning and improvement.

They foster creativity and innovation: Open-ended questions can spark new ideas and approaches that might not have been considered otherwise.

They build trust and engagement: When leaders ask for input, team members feel valued and are more likely to be engaged in their work.

They improve decision-making: Questions help gather diverse perspectives, leading to more informed and well-rounded decisions.

They develop critical thinking skills: By asking thought-provoking questions, leaders help their team members develop problem-solving abilities.

Types of Questions Leaders Should Ask

Different situations call for different types of questions. Here are some categories of questions that leaders can use:

Open-ended questions: These encourage detailed responses and can lead to new insights. For example: "What do you think are the main challenges we face in this project?"

Clarifying questions: These help ensure everyone is on the same page. For example: "Can you explain what you mean by 'streamline the process'?"

Probing questions: These dig deeper into a topic to uncover underlying issues or opportunities. For example: "What factors do you think contributed to the success of our last campaign?"

Hypothetical questions: These explore potential scenarios and encourage creative thinking. For example: "If we had unlimited resources, how would you approach this problem?"

Reflective questions: These promote self-awareness and learning from experience. For example: "What did you learn from this situation that you can apply in the future?"

How to Ask Effective Questions

Asking good questions is a skill that can be developed. Here are some tips for asking effective questions:

Be genuinely curious: Show real interest in the answers. Your team will notice if you're just going through the motions.

Listen actively: Pay attention to the responses and ask follow-up questions based on what you hear.

Use simple language: Avoid jargon or complicated terms that might confuse or intimidate team members.

Be specific: Vague questions often lead to vague answers. Be clear about what you're asking.

Allow time for thought: Give people time to consider their responses. Silence can be productive.

Avoid leading questions: Don't phrase questions in a way that suggests the answer you want to hear.

Be open to unexpected answers: Sometimes the most valuable insights come from responses you didn't anticipate.

Creating a Question-Friendly Environment

For questions to be effective, leaders need to create an environment where people feel comfortable asking and answering questions. Here are some ways to do this:

Model the behavior: Ask questions yourself and show that it's okay not to have all the answers.

Encourage questions: Regularly invite team members to ask questions and share their thoughts.

Respond positively: Even if a question seems off-base, respond in a way that encourages further discussion.

Make it safe to challenge: Create an atmosphere where people feel comfortable questioning the status quo or challenging ideas respectfully.

Use questions in meetings: Structure meetings around key questions to encourage participation and focused discussion.

Reward curiosity: Recognize and praise team members who ask insightful questions or contribute valuable ideas.

Leading Through Questions: Practical Applications

Here are some specific ways leaders can use questions to guide their teams:

Setting goals and objectives: Instead of dictating goals, ask questions like:

"What do you think our main priorities should be for the next quarter?"

"How can we measure our success in achieving these goals?"

"What obstacles do you foresee in reaching these objectives?"

Problem-solving: When faced with challenges, use questions to involve the team in finding solutions:

"What do you think is the root cause of this issue?"

"What potential solutions can we consider?"

"How have we solved similar problems in the past?"

Performance reviews: Use questions to make performance discussions more productive:

"What accomplishments are you most proud of?"

"Where do you see opportunities for growth?"

"How can I better support you in your role?"

Team building: Strengthen team relationships with questions that promote understanding:

"What motivates you in your work?"

"How do you prefer to receive feedback?"

"What skills or experiences do you bring to the team that we might not be fully utilizing?"

Innovation and improvement: Encourage creative thinking with questions like:

"If we were starting this project from scratch today, what would we do differently?"

"What trends in our industry should we be paying more attention to?"

"How can we make our processes more efficient?"

Decision-making: Involve the team in important decisions by asking:

"What are the pros and cons of each option?"

"What potential risks should we consider?"

"Who else might be affected by this decision, and how?"

Empowering Teams with Questions

When leaders use questions effectively, they empower their teams in several ways:

Developing problem-solving skills: By asking questions instead of providing immediate solutions, leaders help team members develop their own problem-solving abilities.

Encouraging ownership: When team members contribute to decisions and solutions through their responses to questions, they feel a greater sense of ownership and responsibility.

Promoting critical thinking: Thoughtful questions challenge team members to analyze situations more deeply and consider multiple perspectives.

Fostering independence: As team members become more comfortable answering questions and thinking through challenges, they become less reliant on the leader for direction.

Building confidence: Successfully answering challenging questions and contributing valuable insights boosts team members' confidence in their abilities.

Encouraging collaboration: Questions that require input from multiple team members promote collaboration and the sharing of diverse viewpoints.

Overcoming Challenges in Leading with Questions

While leading through questions can be powerful, it's not without challenges. Here are some common obstacles and how to address them:

Resistance to change: Some team members might be uncomfortable with a leader who asks questions instead of giving directives. Address this by explaining the benefits of this approach and gradually introducing more question-based leadership.

Time constraints: In fast-paced environments, it might seem quicker to just give orders. However, investing time in asking questions often leads to better long-term results and more efficient problem-solving.

Lack of trust: If team members don't trust the leader or fear negative consequences, they might be hesitant to answer honestly. Build trust by consistently showing that you value their input and using it constructively.

Overuse of questions: Asking too many questions or using them in inappropriate situations can be counterproductive. Balance question-asking with other forms of communication and leadership.

Difficulty framing effective questions: It takes practice to ask good questions. Continually work on improving your questioning skills and seek feedback on their effectiveness.

Leading through questions is a powerful approach that can transform how leaders interact with their teams. By asking thoughtful questions, leaders can guide their teams towards better solutions, foster a culture of learning and innovation, and empower team members to develop their skills and confidence. While it requires practice and patience, the benefits of this approach are substantial. As leaders become more skilled at using questions, they'll find that their teams become more engaged, creative, and capable of tackling complex challenges. In today's rapidly changing business environment, the ability to ask the right questions at the right time is perhaps one of the

most valuable skills a leader can possess.

# Enhancing Learning Through Questions

Questions are powerful tools in education. They can spark curiosity, encourage deeper thinking, and help students understand complex ideas. This chapter looks at how questions can improve learning and build critical thinking skills in educational settings.

The Importance of Questions in Learning

Questions do more than just check what students know. They can:

Get students interested in a topic

Make students think about what they already know

Help students see connections between ideas

Encourage students to look at things from different angles

Show gaps in understanding that need to be filled

When teachers and students ask good questions, it can make learning more active and engaging. Instead of just listening and memorizing facts, students have to think carefully and come up with their own ideas.

Types of Questions in Education

There are many ways to group different kinds of questions. One common way is to split them into lower-order and higher-order questions:

Lower-order questions:

Ask for basic facts or definitions

Can often be answered with a simple yes or no

Test memory and recall

Examples:

What is the capital of France?

When did World War II end?

Who wrote "Romeo and Juliet"?

Higher-order questions:

Require deeper thinking and analysis

Often have more than one possible answer

Ask students to apply, evaluate, or create

Examples:

How might history be different if the Allied powers had lost World War II?

What are the pros and cons of using renewable energy sources?

How would you design a city to be more environmentally friendly?

Both types of questions are useful in education. Lower-order questions can check basic understanding, while higher-order questions push students to think more deeply.

Bloom's Taxonomy and Questioning

Bloom's Taxonomy is a well-known framework in education that organizes thinking skills from simple to complex. It can be a helpful tool for creating different types of questions:

Remember: Questions that ask students to recall facts
Example: What are the parts of a plant cell?

Understand: Questions that check if students grasp the meaning of information Example: Can you explain photosynthesis in your own words?

Apply: Questions that ask students to use information in new situations Example: How would you use this math formula to solve a real-world problem?

Analyze: Questions that ask students to break information into parts and see relationships Example: What are the main causes of climate change, and how do they relate to each other?

Evaluate: Questions that ask students to judge the value of ideas or materials Example: Which of these two experiments do you think gives more reliable results, and why?

Create: Questions that ask students to put elements together to form something new Example: How would you design an experiment to test this scientific theory?

By using questions from all levels of Bloom's Taxonomy, teachers can help students develop a range of thinking skills.

Strategies for Effective Questioning in the Classroom

Wait Time: After asking a question, teachers should wait 3-5 seconds before calling on someone. This gives all students time to think and form an answer.

No Hands Rule: Instead of having students raise their hands, teachers can call on students randomly. This keeps everyone engaged and thinking about the question.

Follow-up Questions: When a student answers, ask them to explain their thinking or give examples. This pushes them to think more deeply.

Student-Generated Questions: Encourage students to come up with their own questions about the topic. This helps them engage more actively with the material.

Think-Pair-Share: After asking a question, have students think about it alone, then discuss with a partner, and finally share with the whole class.

Open-Ended Questions: Use questions that have multiple possible answers to encourage discussion and creative thinking.

Scaffolding: Start with simpler questions and gradually increase the difficulty to build students' confidence and skills.

Developing Students' Questioning Skills

Teaching students how to ask good questions is just as important as teaching them how to answer them. Here are some ways to help students become better at asking questions:

Model Good Questions: Teachers can show students what good questions look like by asking thoughtful questions themselves.

Question Formulation Technique: This is a step-by-step process that helps students learn to ask their own questions:

Choose a topic

Have students generate as many questions as they can about it

Improve the questions by changing them from closed (yes/no) to open-ended or vice versa

Prioritize the questions

Plan how to use the questions

Socratic Circles: In this activity, students sit in two circles. The inner circle discusses a topic, while the outer circle listens and then asks questions about the discussion.

Question Boards: Create a space in the classroom where students can post questions about what they're learning.

Research Projects: Have students come up with their own research questions for projects, then guide them in refining these questions.

Peer Questioning: During group work, have students take turns asking each other questions about the topic they're studying.

Questions and Critical Thinking

Critical thinking is the ability to analyze information, see different perspectives, and make reasoned judgments. Questions play a key role in developing these skills:

Analysis Questions: These help students break down complex ideas. Example: What are the main arguments in this article?

Comparison Questions: These encourage students to see similarities and differences. Example: How is this character similar to or different from the one we studied last week?

Perspective-Taking Questions: These push students to look at issues from different angles. Example: How might this historical event be viewed differently by people from different countries?

Evaluation Questions: These ask students to make judgments based on criteria. Example: Which of these solutions do you think would be most effective, and why?

Hypothetical Questions: These help students imagine different scenarios and outcomes. Example: What might happen if this law were changed?

By regularly asking and answering these types of questions, students can improve their critical thinking skills over time.

Challenges in Using Questions Effectively

While questions are powerful learning tools, there can be challenges in using them well:

Uneven Participation: Some students may dominate discussions while others stay quiet.

Surface-Level Thinking: If questions are too easy, students might not engage deeply with the material.

Fear of Being Wrong: Some students might be afraid to answer if they're not sure they're right.

Misunderstanding the Question: Students might give off-topic answers if they don't understand what's being asked.

Time Constraints: In-depth questioning can take a lot of class time, which can be challenging with packed curricula.

To address these challenges, teachers can:

Use a mix of individual, small group, and whole class questioning

Provide scaffolding to help students tackle harder questions

Create a classroom culture where mistakes are seen as learning opportunities

Rephrase questions if students seem confused

Plan questioning carefully to use class time effectively

Conclusion

Questions are essential tools for learning and thinking. By using a variety of question types, teaching students to ask good questions, and creating a classroom environment that values inquiry, educators can greatly enhance learning and help students develop critical thinking skills. As students become better at asking and answering questions, they become more active, engaged learners who are better prepared to think critically about the world around them.

# Understanding Client Needs

Effective questioning is a key skill in sales and negotiation. By asking the right questions, you can understand your clients' needs, build rapport, and guide them towards making decisions that benefit both parties. This chapter explores how to use questions strategically throughout the sales process, from initial contact to closing the deal.

The Power of Questions in Sales

Questions are more than just tools for gathering information. They:

Show interest in the client

Help you understand the client's situation and needs

Make the client feel heard and valued

Guide the conversation in productive directions

Help the client discover their own motivations and priorities

Create opportunities to present your solutions effectively

## Types of Questions for Different Stages of the Sales Process

### Opening Questions

These questions start the conversation and build rapport. They should be open-ended and easy to answer:

"How's your day going so far?"

"What made you interested in our products/services?"

"What's currently working well in your business?"

### Situation Questions

Use these to understand the client's current state:

"Can you tell me about your current process for [relevant task]?"

"What tools or systems are you using now?"

"How long have you been dealing with [specific issue]?"

Problem Questions

These questions uncover pain points and challenges:

"What difficulties are you facing with your current approach?"

"How is [specific issue] affecting your business?"

"What would happen if this problem isn't solved?"

Implication Questions

These questions help the client see the full impact of their problems:

"How does this issue affect your team's productivity?"

"What's the financial impact of this problem on your business?"

"How might this problem grow if left unaddressed?"

Need-Payoff Questions

These questions get the client thinking about the benefits of solving their problem:

"How would solving this issue impact your business?"

"What would it mean for your team if you could [achieve specific goal]?"

"If you could wave a magic wand and fix this, what would the ideal outcome look like?"

Qualifying Questions

Use these to determine if the client is a good fit for your offering:

"What's your budget for this project?"

"Who else is involved in the decision-making process?"

"What's your timeline for implementing a solution?"

Techniques for Effective Questioning

Use Open-Ended Questions

Open-ended questions encourage detailed responses and give you more information to work with. Instead of asking, "Do you like your current supplier?" try "What has your experience been like with your current supplier?"

### Listen Actively

Pay close attention to the client's responses. Take notes if needed. Show you're listening through body language and verbal cues.

### Follow Up

Based on the client's answers, ask follow-up questions to dig deeper. This shows you're engaged and helps you gather more useful information.

### Use Silence

After asking a question, give the client time to think and respond. Don't rush to fill silences – they often lead to more thoughtful answers.

### Avoid Leading Questions

Don't ask questions that push the client towards a specific answer. For example, instead of "Don't you think our product would solve your problem?" ask "How do you think our product might fit into your process?"

Be Curious

Approach each client with genuine curiosity. Your goal is to truly understand their situation, not just to set up your sales pitch.

Understanding Client Needs Through Questioning

To truly understand your client's needs, you need to go beyond surface-level information. Use a mix of question types to build a complete picture:

Current Situation: "What's your current process for [relevant task]?"

Goals: "What are you hoping to achieve in the next year?"

Challenges: "What obstacles are preventing you from reaching those goals?"

Past Attempts: "Have you tried to solve this problem before? What happened?"

Decision Criteria: "What factors will you consider when choosing a solution?"

Ideal Outcome: "If we were having this conversation a year from now, what would success look like?"

By asking these types of questions, you'll gain a deep understanding of your client's needs, allowing you to tailor your approach and offer more relevant solutions.

Closing Deals with Strategic Questions

As you move towards closing the deal, your questions should guide the client towards making a decision. Here are some effective closing questions:

Confirmation Questions

"Based on what we've discussed, does our solution seem like a good fit for your needs?"

"Do you see how this could solve [specific problem we discussed]?"

Next Steps Questions

"What do you think should be our next steps?"

"When would you like to start implementing this solution?"

Objection-Surfacing Questions

"Is there anything that might prevent you from moving forward with this?"

"What concerns do you have that we haven't addressed yet?"

Commitment Questions

"Are you ready to move forward with this solution?"

"Shall we prepare the agreement for your review?"

Alternative Close Questions

"Would you prefer to start with the basic package or the premium option?"

"Should we schedule the implementation for next month or the month after?"

Summary Close Questions

"We've covered a lot today. Can I summarize the key points to make sure we're on the same page?"

"Based on everything we've discussed, do you agree that this solution meets your needs?"

Remember, the goal isn't to pressure the client but to help them make a confident decision. If they're not ready to commit, use questions to understand their hesitation and address any remaining concerns.

Common Mistakes to Avoid

Asking Too Many Closed Questions: These limit the information you receive and can make the conversation feel like an interrogation.

Not Listening to the Answers: If you're too focused on your next question, you might miss important information or opportunities to dig deeper.

Asking Multiple Questions at Once: This can confuse the client and lead to incomplete answers.

Using Jargon or Complex Language: Keep your questions clear and simple to ensure the client understands and can respond effectively.

Neglecting Emotional Aspects: Don't focus solely on facts and figures. Ask questions that uncover the client's feelings and motivations.

Failing to Adapt: If your prepared questions aren't working, be ready to change your approach based on the client's responses.

Conclusion

Mastering the art of questioning is a powerful way to improve your sales and negotiation skills. By asking the right questions at the right time, you can understand your clients better, build stronger relationships, and guide conversations towards mutually beneficial outcomes. Remember, the goal isn't just to make a sale, but to find the best solution for your client's needs. With practice and patience, you can turn every sales conversation into an opportunity for discovery and problem-solving.

# Building a Questioning Mindset

In our journey to master the art of questioning, we must first develop a mindset that values and promotes inquiry. This chapter explores how to build such a mindset, nurture curiosity, and use questions as tools for ongoing personal and professional growth.

The Questioning Mindset

A questioning mindset is a way of thinking that prioritizes inquiry, exploration, and learning. It's about being open to new ideas, challenging assumptions, and seeking to understand the world around us more deeply. People with a questioning mindset don't just accept things at face value; they dig deeper, ask why, and look for connections and patterns.

To develop a questioning mindset, start by:

Staying open-minded: Be willing to consider new ideas and perspectives, even if they challenge your existing beliefs.

Practicing active listening: Pay close attention to what others are saying, and ask follow-up questions to gain a better understanding.

Suspending judgment: Avoid jumping to conclusions too quickly. Instead, gather more information through thoughtful questions.

Accepting uncertainty: Recognize that it's okay not to have all the answers. Use questions as a way to navigate uncertainty and learn more.

Valuing learning over being right: Focus on gaining knowledge and understanding rather than proving yourself correct.

Challenging assumptions: Question your own beliefs and those of others. Ask, "Why do we think this way?" or "What evidence supports this idea?"

Seeking diverse perspectives: Ask questions of people with different backgrounds, experiences, and viewpoints to broaden your understanding.

Cultivating Curiosity

Curiosity is the fuel that drives a questioning mindset. It's the desire to learn, explore, and understand the world around us. Curious people are naturally inclined to ask questions and seek out new information. Here are some ways to cultivate curiosity:

Follow your interests: Pay attention to topics that genuinely interest you. Ask questions about these subjects and pursue answers.

Read widely: Expose yourself to various subjects through books, articles, and other media. This can spark new questions and areas of interest.

Try new experiences: Step out of your comfort zone and try new activities. This can lead to fresh questions and insights.

Practice mindfulness: Pay attention to your surroundings and the present moment. Notice details you might typically overlook, and ask questions about what you observe.

Play with ideas: Allow yourself to think creatively and imagine "what if" scenarios. This can lead to interesting questions and new ways of thinking.

Connect with curious people: Surround yourself with individuals who ask thoughtful questions and enjoy learning. Their curiosity can be contagious.

Keep a question journal: Write down questions that come to mind throughout the day. Review them later and consider how you might find answers.

Use technology wisely: Use online resources to explore topics that interest you, but be careful not to let quick answers replace deep thinking and questioning.

Embrace the unknown: View gaps in your knowledge as opportunities for learning rather than as weaknesses.

Ask "why" and "how": Go beyond surface-level information by asking about underlying reasons and processes.

Continuous Improvement Through Questioning

Questions are powerful tools for personal and professional growth. They help us identify areas for improvement, gain new insights, and solve problems more effectively. Here's how you can use questions to drive continuous improvement:

Self-reflection: Regularly ask yourself questions about your goals, values, and actions. For example:

What did I learn today?

How can I improve my skills in [specific area]?

Am I living up to my values? If not, why?

What's holding me back from achieving my goals?

Feedback seeking: Ask others for their input and perspectives. Some useful questions include:

What do you think I could do better?

How do you see my strengths and weaknesses?

Can you give me an example of when I [specific behavior]?

What would make our work together more effective?

Problem-solving: Use questions to break down complex issues and find solutions:

What's the root cause of this problem?

What assumptions am I making about this situation?

What alternative solutions haven't I considered?

How have others solved similar problems?

Goal setting: Ask questions to clarify your objectives and create actionable plans:

What specifically do I want to achieve?

Why is this goal important to me?

What steps do I need to take to reach this goal?

How will I measure my progress?

Learning from failures: When things don't go as planned, ask:

What went wrong and why?

What can I learn from this experience?

How can I prevent similar issues in the future?

What would I do differently next time?

Challenging the status quo: To drive innovation and improvement, ask:

Why do we do things this way?

What would happen if we tried a different approach?

How can we make this process more efficient?

What needs of our customers/users aren't we meeting?

Expanding knowledge: To continue learning and growing, ask:

What don't I know about this topic?

Where can I find reliable information on this subject?

Who are the experts in this field, and what can I learn from them?

How does this new information connect to what I already know?

Developing empathy: To better understand others and improve relationships, ask:

How does this person feel about the situation?

What motivates their actions or decisions?

How can I better support or communicate with this person?

What can I learn from their perspective?

Time management: To improve productivity and focus, ask:

Is this task the best use of my time right now?

How can I eliminate or reduce time-wasting activities?

What tasks should I prioritize to have the biggest impact?

How can I create more time for important but non-urgent activities?

Ethical decision-making: When facing moral dilemmas, ask:

What are the potential consequences of each option?

How does this decision align with my values and principles?

Who will be affected by this decision, and how?

What would a person I admire do in this situation?

Putting It All Together: The Questioning Cycle

To truly build a questioning mindset, cultivate curiosity, and drive continuous improvement, it's helpful to think of questioning as an ongoing cycle:

Observe: Pay attention to your surroundings, experiences, and inner thoughts.

Wonder: Allow curiosity to arise naturally from your observations.

Ask: Formulate questions based on what you're curious about.

Seek: Look for answers through research, experimentation, or asking others.

Reflect: Think about what you've learned and how it fits with your existing knowledge.

Apply: Use your new understanding to take action or make decisions.

Evaluate: Assess the results of your actions and decisions.

Repeat: Begin the cycle again with new observations and questions.

By engaging in this questioning cycle regularly, you'll develop a habit of inquiry that leads to ongoing learning and growth.

Overcoming Barriers to Questioning

Even with the best intentions, you may encounter obstacles to maintaining a questioning mindset. Here are some common barriers and how to overcome them:

Fear of appearing ignorant: Remember that asking questions shows a desire to learn, not a lack of intelligence. Reframe questions as a sign of engagement and curiosity.

Time constraints: Prioritize important questions and build time for reflection into your schedule. Even brief moments of inquiry can be valuable.

Information overload: Focus on asking high-quality questions rather than trying to question everything. Develop the skill of identifying which questions are most important or relevant.

Lack of practice: Like any skill, questioning improves with practice. Make a conscious effort to ask more questions in your daily life, both of yourself and others.

Closed-minded environments: If you're in a setting that discourages questions, seek out other spaces or communities where inquiry is valued. Online forums, book clubs, or professional networks can provide supportive environments for questioning.

Building a questioning mindset, cultivating curiosity, and using questions for continuous improvement are interconnected processes that can greatly enrich your life and work. By staying open-minded, nurturing your natural curiosity, and consistently asking thoughtful questions, you'll gain deeper understanding, solve problems more effectively, and continue to grow personally and professionally.

Remember, the art of questioning is not about having all the answers, but about knowing how to ask the right questions at the right time. As you continue to develop your questioning skills, you'll find that the world becomes a more fascinating and opportunity-filled place, with each question opening new doors to learning and growth.

# Overcoming Common Mistakes

Asking good questions is a skill that can be improved with practice and awareness. Many people make common mistakes when asking questions, but by understanding these pitfalls and learning how to avoid them, you can become a more effective questioner. This chapter will explore some of the most frequent errors people make when asking questions and provide practical advice on how to overcome them.

Asking Closed-Ended Questions When Open-Ended Ones Are Needed

One of the most common mistakes in questioning is using closed-ended questions when open-ended ones would be more appropriate. Closed-ended questions typically elicit short, specific answers, often just "yes" or "no." While these questions have their place, they can limit the depth and breadth of information you receive.

Example of a closed-ended question: "Did you enjoy the movie?" Better open-ended alternative: "What did you think about the movie?"

The open-ended version allows the respondent to share their thoughts and feelings more fully, potentially leading to a richer conversation.

How to avoid this pitfall:

Before asking a question, consider what type of information you're seeking.

If you want detailed responses or to start a discussion, use open-ended questions.

Practice rephrasing closed-ended questions into open-ended ones.

Asking Leading Questions

Leading questions are those that suggest or prompt a specific answer. They can be problematic because they may bias the respondent's answer or make them feel pressured to respond in a certain way.

Example of a leading question: "Don't you think the new policy is unfair?" Better neutral alternative: "What are your thoughts on the new policy?"

The neutral version allows the respondent to share their honest opinion without feeling guided toward a particular response.

How to avoid this pitfall:

Be aware of your own biases and try to phrase questions neutrally.

Ask yourself if your question allows for all possible answers, not just the one you might expect or prefer.

Have someone else review your questions if you're preparing for an important interview or survey.

Asking Multiple Questions at Once

Asking multiple questions in a single breath can overwhelm the respondent and lead to incomplete or confused answers. It's often called "double-barreled" questioning when two questions are combined into one.

Example of multiple questions: "How did you like the presentation, and what improvements would you suggest for next time?" Better approach: Ask these as two separate questions.

By separating the questions, you allow the respondent to focus on one aspect at a time, potentially leading to more thoughtful and comprehensive answers.

How to avoid this pitfall:

Break down complex inquiries into individual questions.

Ask one question at a time and wait for the response before moving to the next.

If you find yourself wanting to ask multiple questions, prioritize the most important one to ask first.

Using Vague or Ambiguous Language

Unclear or imprecise language in questions can lead to confusion and misinterpretation. When questions are vague, respondents may not understand what information you're seeking, resulting in unhelpful answers.

Example of a vague question: "How was it?" Clearer alternative: "How did you find the customer service experience at the store today?"

The clearer version provides context and specifies exactly what aspect you're inquiring about.

How to avoid this pitfall:

Be specific about what you're asking.

Use clear, concrete language.

Provide context if necessary to ensure the question is understood as intended.

Asking Overly Complex Questions

Questions that are too complicated or contain too many parts can be difficult for respondents to understand and answer effectively. This is especially true in verbal communication, where the respondent can't refer back to a written question.

Example of a complex question: "Considering the current economic climate, recent policy changes, and potential future market trends, how do you think small businesses in the tech sector will adapt their strategies over the next five years?" Simplified alternative: "How do you think small tech businesses will change their strategies in the coming years?"

The simplified version is easier to process and answer, while still capturing the essence of the inquiry.

How to avoid this pitfall:

Keep questions simple and straightforward.

If a complex topic needs to be addressed, break it down into several simpler questions.

Consider the knowledge level of your audience and adjust the complexity accordingly.

Not Allowing Enough Time for Responses

In conversations or interviews, it's common for questioners to rush to the next question without giving the respondent enough time to think and answer fully. This can result in shallow or incomplete responses.

How to avoid this pitfall:

Practice active listening and be comfortable with silence.

Give the respondent time to think before answering.

If the person seems to have more to say, wait a moment before moving on to the next question.

Asking Questions That Are Too Personal or Sensitive

Depending on the context and your relationship with the respondent, some questions may be too personal or sensitive. Asking such questions can make people uncomfortable and unwilling to engage further.

Example of a too personal question: "Why did you and your ex-partner break up?" Better alternative: "How have you been doing lately?"

The alternative question shows concern without prying into potentially sensitive areas.

How to avoid this pitfall:

Consider the appropriateness of your questions given the context and your relationship with the respondent.

Start with less personal questions and only move to more sensitive topics if the respondent seems comfortable and willing.

Respect boundaries and be prepared to back off if the person seems uncomfortable.

Not Following Up on Answers

Sometimes, the initial answer to a question may be brief or unclear. Failing to follow up in these cases can mean missing out on valuable information or insights.

How to avoid this pitfall:

Listen carefully to responses and be ready to ask follow-up questions for clarification or more detail.

Use prompts like "Can you tell me more about that?" or "What do you mean by...?" to encourage elaboration.

Practice active listening techniques to ensure you're fully engaging with the responses you receive.

Asking Questions That Assume Knowledge

Asking questions that assume the respondent has certain knowledge or experience can lead to confusion or embarrassment if they don't have that background.

Example of a question assuming knowledge: "What do you think about the new quantum computing breakthrough?" Better alternative: "Are you familiar with recent developments in quantum computing? If so, what are your thoughts on them?"

The alternative version first checks if the person has the necessary knowledge before asking for their opinion.

How to avoid this pitfall:

Assess the likely knowledge level of your audience before formulating questions.

When in doubt, provide context or background information as part of your question.

Be prepared to explain concepts if the respondent isn't familiar with them.

Not Considering the Impact of Your Questions

Questions can have emotional or psychological impacts on respondents. Failing to consider these potential effects can lead to unintended consequences or damaged relationships.

How to avoid this pitfall:

Think about how your questions might be perceived or felt by the respondent.

Consider the potential consequences of asking certain questions, especially in sensitive situations.

Be prepared to offer support or resources if your questions touch on difficult topics.

Learning from Experience

Improving your questioning skills is an ongoing process that involves learning from your experiences. Here are some strategies to help you grow:

Reflect on Your Conversations: After important discussions or interviews, take time to think about what went well and what could have been improved in your questioning approach.

Seek Feedback: Ask trusted colleagues, friends, or mentors to provide feedback on your questioning techniques. They may notice patterns or issues that you've overlooked.

Practice Active Listening: Good questioning often involves listening carefully to responses and using that information to guide your next questions. Work on your listening skills alongside your questioning skills.

Study Effective Questioners: Pay attention to skilled interviewers, teachers, or leaders. Notice how they structure their questions and interact with respondents.

Keep a Question Journal: Write down questions that you find particularly effective or that lead to interesting discussions. Analyze why they worked well and how you might adapt them for future use.

Experiment with Different Techniques: Try out various questioning strategies in low-stakes situations to see what works best for you and in different contexts.

Be Patient with Yourself: Remember that developing strong questioning skills takes time and practice. Be kind to yourself as you learn and grow.

By being aware of these common pitfalls and actively working to avoid them, you can significantly improve your questioning skills. Remember that asking good questions is not just about getting information; it's about fostering understanding, encouraging thoughtful responses, and building meaningful connections with others. As you continue to practice and learn from your experiences, you'll find that your ability to ask effective questions will grow, leading to more insightful conversations and better outcomes in various aspects of your life.

# Becoming a Questioning Expert

As you progress in your journey to become a questioning expert, it's important to move beyond basic techniques and explore more advanced methods. This chapter will examine real-world examples and case studies that show how skilled questioners use advanced techniques to gain deeper insights, solve complex problems, and drive meaningful change.

Advanced Questioning Techniques

The Socratic Method

The Socratic method involves asking a series of questions to help others uncover their assumptions, examine their beliefs, and reach new conclusions. This technique is particularly useful in educational settings and philosophical discussions.

Case Study: Philosophy Class Professor Maria Chen uses the Socratic method in her undergraduate philosophy class to help students think critically about ethical dilemmas. When discussing the trolley problem, she asks:

"What do you think is the right action in this scenario?"

"Why do you believe that's the correct choice?"

"How would your decision change if the circumstances were slightly different?"

"What underlying principles are guiding your reasoning?"

By asking these probing questions, Professor Chen helps her students explore their own moral reasoning and uncover the complexities of ethical decision-making.

The Five Whys

This technique involves asking "why" repeatedly to get to the root cause of a problem. It's commonly used in business and engineering to identify the underlying issues behind surface-level problems.

Case Study: Manufacturing Company A manufacturing company was experiencing frequent product defects. The quality control manager, John Smith, used the Five Whys technique to identify the root cause:

Why are we seeing so many defects? Because the parts don't fit together properly.

Why don't the parts fit together properly? Because they're not made to the correct specifications.

Why aren't they made to the correct specifications? Because the machines are not calibrated correctly.

Why aren't the machines calibrated correctly? Because the calibration process is not standardized.

Why isn't the calibration process standardized? Because we haven't updated our procedures since getting new equipment.

By asking these questions, John identified that the root cause was outdated calibration procedures, which led to a solution that significantly reduced defects.

Appreciative Inquiry

This technique focuses on asking positive questions to identify strengths and opportunities rather than weaknesses and problems. It's often used in organizational development and change management.

Case Study: Non-Profit Organization A struggling non-profit organization hired consultant Sarah Jones to help improve their operations. Instead of focusing on what was going wrong, Sarah used appreciative inquiry:

"When was a time the organization was at its best?"

"What factors contributed to that success?"

"How can we build on those strengths?"

"What opportunities do you see for the future?"

By asking these positive questions, Sarah helped the organization identify its core strengths and develop a plan for growth based on past successes.

Circular Questioning

This technique, often used in family therapy, involves asking questions about the relationships and interactions between people rather than about individuals themselves.

Case Study: Family Therapy Therapist David Lee used circular questioning to help a family struggling with communication issues:

To the mother: "How do you think your daughter feels when your husband raises his voice?"

To the father: "What do you notice about your wife's behavior when your son stays out late?"

To the son: "How do you think your sister reacts when you and your mother argue?"

By asking these questions, David helped the family members gain new perspectives on their interactions and patterns of behavior.

The Funnel Technique

This approach involves starting with broad, open-ended questions and gradually narrowing down to more specific, detailed inquiries. It's often used in market research and customer interviews.

Case Study: Product Development Product manager Lisa Chen used the funnel technique to gather insights for a new smartphone app:

Broad: "How do you typically manage your daily tasks?" Narrower: "What tools or apps do you currently use for task management?" More specific: "What features do you find most useful in these apps?" Detailed: "How often do you use the reminder function in your current task management app?"

By using this technique, Lisa gathered comprehensive information about user needs and preferences, which informed the development of a more user-friendly app.

Real-World Applications of Advanced Questioning Techniques

Criminal Investigations

Detective Alex Rodriguez uses a combination of open-ended and closed-ended questions when interviewing suspects and witnesses. He starts with broad questions to get the subject talking, then uses more specific follow-up questions to clarify details and identify inconsistencies.

## Scientific Research

Dr. Emily Watson, a climate scientist, uses hypothetical questions to explore possible future scenarios. She asks questions like, "What would happen to sea levels if global temperatures rise by 2 degrees Celsius?" These questions help her team model potential outcomes and develop mitigation strategies.

## Business Strategy

CEO Michael Brown uses probing questions in board meetings to challenge assumptions and push for innovative thinking. He often asks, "What if we're wrong about this?" or "How would our competitors approach this problem?" These questions encourage his team to consider alternative perspectives and strategies.

## Journalism

Investigative journalist Rachel Green uses a combination of factual and interpretive questions when conducting interviews. She asks for specific facts and figures, but also probes for the subject's opinions and interpretations of events. This approach helps her uncover both the facts of a story and the human elements behind it.

Medical Diagnosis

Dr. James Lee uses a structured questioning approach when diagnosing patients. He starts with open-ended questions about symptoms, then asks more specific follow-up questions based on the patient's responses. This method helps him gather comprehensive information and avoid missing crucial details.

The most effective questioners are those who listen carefully, adapt their techniques to the situation, and remain curious and open-minded. With practice and persistence, you can become a master of the art of questioning, unlocking new levels of understanding and insight in both your personal and professional life.

# Conclusion

Questioning is not a skill we master once and forget. It's a practice we keep developing throughout our lives. As we've seen in this book, the art of questioning involves many aspects - from understanding different types of questions to knowing when and how to ask them effectively.

Our world is always changing, bringing new challenges and opportunities. This means we always have more to learn and understand. By continuing to ask questions, we keep growing and adapting.

Great questioners are not born - they're made through practice and reflection. Every time you ask a question, you have a chance to improve your skills. Pay attention to how people respond to your questions. Notice which questions lead to helpful answers and which ones don't work as well. Learn from your experiences and keep trying new approaches.

It's also important to stay curious. Curiosity is the fuel that drives good questions. Make an effort to stay interested in the world around you. Read widely, talk to different people, and explore new ideas. The more you know, the more questions you'll be able to ask.

Don't be afraid to question your own beliefs and assumptions. Self-reflection is a key part of the questioning journey. Regularly ask yourself why you think the way you do. This can help you uncover biases and broaden your perspective.

Questioning is not just about getting answers. It's also about sparking new ideas, starting conversations, and encouraging deeper thinking. Sometimes, a good question is valuable even if it doesn't have a clear answer.

As you continue your journey, keep in mind that becoming a skilled questioner takes time. Be patient with yourself. Celebrate your progress, but always look for ways to improve. The art of questioning is a lifelong practice, and there's always more to learn.

A.  *Please scan the books series*
*"Super Power".*

B.  *Please scan the books series*
*"Life Mastery".*

C.  *Please scan the book series,*
*"The Art of Living"*